D1242221

DOORS

1

2

3

4

5

6

7

8

9

If a man write a better book, preach a better sermon, or make a better mousetrap than his neighbor, though he build his house in the woods, the world will make a beaten path to his door.

Ralph Waldo Emerson

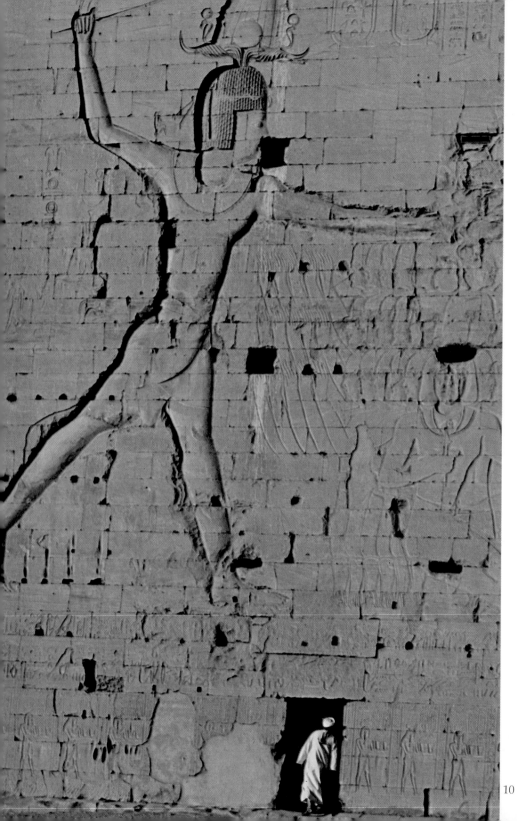

10

DOORS

Text by Val Clery

Photographs by Gordon Beck, John Bigg,
Bill Brooks, John de Visser, Peter Dominick,
Ted Grant, Rudi Haas, Jennifer Harper, G.J. Harris,
Uta Hoffmann, Charles Kadin, Fiona Mee, Bill McLaughlin
Barry Moscrop, Wim Noordhoek, Murray Sumner and
Robert van der Hilst

A Jonathan-James Book

Macmillan of Canada, Toronto

Canadian Cataloguing in Publication Data

Clery, Val, 1924-
  Doors

"A Jonathan-James book"

ISBN 0-7705-1737-4 pa.

1. Doors. 2. Doorways. 3. Photography, Artistic.
I. Beck, Gordon.

TR654.C54   779'.4   C78-001303-4

Printed in the United States for
The Macmillan Company of Canada Limited
70 Bond Street
Toronto M5B 1X3

If windows are the eyes of a house, a door is its mouth. Windows are passive, doors are active. Through windows we glimpse what is and what happens, but when we pass through a doorway we encounter and most likely become involved in what lies beyond.

Doors remain closed to tell us of our rejection or of another's seclusion, doors open to welcome us or to engulf and imprison us, doors frame our farewells or joyful reunions or tearful reconciliations, doors slam like periods at the end of scenes of anger or frustration or bewilderment, doors beckon us to a haven when the world has become too demanding or wearying or threatening and enclose us in love and warmth and familiarity, guarding us solidly from peril and weather and the unknown. Yet doors admit surprises and delights, fresh air, new friends or long-lost lovers, good news, unexpected gifts, longed-for responses, the quick kindness of neighbors, the regular brisk cheer of the mailman.

The frontier crossings between outside and inside, between social and personal, between public and private, between Them and Us, doors mark out our moments of truth, our points of contact, on their hinges swing our fates, through them we go from one passage of our lives to another, retreating, arriving, departing, returning . . . .

Doors are as old as mankind. Even earliest man as a hunter or nomad knew the need to close off the entrance to his cave or tent against predators or enemies or weather. Barriers of spiney branches, piles of rocks, campfires or animal pelts were the best that could be managed, and even when men began to settle and build permanent shelter, they probably protected their doorways in the same makeshift way. Doorways were only large enough to admit a human being, making them easy to cover and to defend.

The settled life brought about communities and the security of numbers. Remains of the earliest human settlements in Asia Minor show them to have been as closely huddled as any inner city neighborhood today, protected either by an outer wall or by the tortuous maze of pathways that wound between the houses, which needed little more to cover their entrances than a curtain of pelts or woven matting. So simple was the common life that theft had little meaning. There are still tropical societies in Africa, Asia and the Pacific where doors remain mere flimsy screens. Wealth and power demand sturdier doors. And more imposing doorways.

Growing communities eventually arrived at the need for government and religion and defense. Palaces, temples and citadels were the first public buildings. Since such structures were usually set above the common level of the community's buildings, what better means to subdue petitioners, worshippers or attackers than to have them climb an exhausting flight of steps and to confront them then with a doorway of larger than human scale, lavish, mysterious and ornate.

16

According to archaeologists, the building methods devised in those Near Eastern settlements thousands of years ago still influence European architecture today. The raw materials at hand dictated the methods adopted. Initially walls were shaped directly from clay mixed with straw, then the idea of bricks formed from the same materials and baked in the sun offered builders a greater flexibility. Elsewhere, alongside rivers, tall pliable reeds were plentiful and these, bound in thick bundles and embedded upright in the ground, formed the basic structure of the houses, the outsides being later plastered with mud; the tops of the walls of reed were bent inwards and tied together, forming a vaulted roof and, at either end, an arched opening, which could be filled with reed matting or left open as a doorway. It is believed that the arch, the vault, the dome and the column, which are still common in Western architecture, all derive from that primitive structure.

One material that was not plentiful in the Near East was wood, and wood, because it is relatively light and easy to shape, is ideal for making doors. Since wood also disintegrates rapidly, archaeologists can only presume that the first doors consisted of light logs lashed to cross-stays and wedged into doorways when needed. The next innovation was probably the wooden door frame, intended primarily to support the wall above the doorspace but also providing a jamb to which the crude door could be attached. The first hinges were just thongs of rawhide, requiring the door to be lifted bodily when opening or closing it. It was not until rigid metal hinges were conceived that doors were able to pivot freely as they do today.

Doors have remained basically the same ever since, although there have been many refinements of their form. One instance is what

we call the Dutch door, which is divided half-way up to allow the top half to be opened, admitting light and fresh air, while the lower half remains closed, keeping stray livestock out and straying children in. It seems very probable that doors of this kind were in use long before they were attributed to the Dutch.

18

Obviously in cooler northern regions more substantial weatherproof houses were needed. Where trees were plentiful, and had in any case to be cleared off the land for cultivation, wood was the obvious material for building. Log-built houses were the earliest kind in the north, because their construction called only for an axe and a great deal of labor. Doors had to be rough-hewn, but there was a virtue in the necessity since heavy doors were needed to keep out the cold. With hard woods available it was possible to shape wooden hinges that would bear the weight and wooden latches. Later when tempered steel saws became available, it was possible to build lighter houses of plank, and lighter less cumbersome doors.

An essential of a well-built doorway, particularly in the north, was a raised threshold to prevent rain or snow from filtering indoors. Similarly a porch, or at least a roof with deep eaves, was a necessity rather than a luxury.

As communities grew and farmsteads prospered, it was necessary to build bigger entrances to admit herds of livestock and wagons and carts. Iron fittings made it possible to hang and to reinforce such large doors, but they were still unwieldy and liable to sag. The answer to this problem was to divide large doors into two leaves, hinged to opposite doorposts and meeting in the middle of the doorway when closed. By this means even the vast gates of fortified towns and citadels could be managed by a few men. Another refinement was the insertion of another smaller door in one of the leaves through which individual pedestrians could pass. In fortifications it also became common to have a

concealed back entrance called a postern or sally port in addition to the main gateway; from this defending patrols could sally forth to harass besieging forces.

Double doors eventually were to become a mark of prestige and in the nineteenth century were often installed in houses with no practical need for them. Indeed some single leaf doors were built so as to appear to be double doors. Such vanity is not surprising since doors are the central feature of buildings and the obvious means of creating a first impression. As societies grew and became stratified, those who considered themselves important followed the example of public buildings and decorated their doorways with crests and symbols that implied their rank, pedigree or wealth.

22

Whether in the Eastern or the Western worlds the entrances to shrines are usually lavished with excesses of decorative art. Such thresholds are intended, after all, not only to inspire awe in approaching worshippers but to stimulate a sense of exaltation, as the prelude to an encounter with divinity.

In most cases they also mark an alliance between God and Mammon, since their creation has usually depended on the munificence of a wealthy patron. Perhaps, since by tradition the rich have less chance of entering the Kingdom of Heaven than the ordinary meek run of men, those patrons of ecclesiastical art have compensated themselves with the thought that at least they have been enabled to create a heavenly gate on earth.

Wherever they have gone after death, they have had no means of taking such treasures with them, so we can continue to draw inspiration from them.

Religion in our time has lost much of its prestige and power. Whatever shrines are being built these days tend to present us with doorways as blank and uninspiring as the entrances of banks. The wealthy seem to have largely transferred their patronage to the only surviving faith, education, from works of art to the arts of work.

23

24

There were times,
though, when those
who were a power in
the land felt no trace of
modesty about proclaiming it
as clearly as possible. Since
few could read, any knight
who was anybody wore his
heart on his shield,
emblazoned in heraldic
imagery, along with his blood
line, his battle honors and
his family allegiances. His
castle was his home, and
anyone, friend or foe,
approaching his gate had no
excuse for not knowing what
manner of man he had to deal
with.

   Today only tourists pause,
and wonder what it all means.

26

Nobility of course has no monopoly on using its doors to proclaim itself. Monsieur Le Curé within his confessional, behind the closed door that releases sinners from their sins, is as proud of his cross as he would be of any coat-of-arms. He would probably be less than pleased if he were aware that much of the elaborate tracery that graces his door derived originally from pagan symbols, as

27

indeed does his cross.

The medieval craftsman who carved the sunrise motif within the wide arch of a doorway was merely copying a traditional design, unaware that the tradition reached back to those days when men did worship the sun. No more was the Regency gentleman aware that the fanlight installed above his elegant front door enshrined the same solar mythology.

29

30

And did the severe Lutherans, who frown on images and symbols, realize that their plain transom combines the square symbol of Earth with the curving symbol of Heaven; appropriately if not intentionally?

History, belief, and custom impose character on doors as heredity imposes it on human faces.

There can be few of us for whom doors do not have a deep emotional significance. They punctuate our memories. If you can not recall it clearly, you must surely feel within you still the irresistible magnetic pull of what lay beyond every half-open door when you could only crawl about your childhood home. Since then the rebukes or disappointments or shocks or even tragedies that may have awaited you beyond some doors, however balanced by the delights and rewards found beyond others, may have conditioned you to hesitate apprehensively at every door you approach. Fortunately for most of us, first impressions remain strongest: the attraction of doors, half-open or not, remains irresistible.

And of course doors need not necessarily lead to confrontation or adventure or surprise; they may offer us repose or comfort or security, may release us from some constraint or burden, or return us to a condition we have longed for.

Doors are the stuff of dreams. And indeed of nightmares. As the psychoanalyst Carl Jung put it: "The dream is the small hidden door in the deepest and most intimate sanctuary of the soul, which opens into the primeval cosmic night that was soul long before there was a conscious ego and will be soul far beyond what conscious ego could ever reach."

There are doors inside us and outside and if we are too fearful to pass through them we will be prisoners no matter on which side of them we stand.

34

Aside from the world of dreams, there are doors enough in the real world that mystify and puzzle. Doors that seem so broodingly sinister as to suggest themselves as ideal settings for a spine-chilling movie, starkly guarding from the brightness of noon creatures of unimaginable evil, awaiting the moment when the moon rises to creak slowly open . . .

Or doors that could serve as setting for a farce. For a door opening half-way up the wall of a house, there is a mundane explanation. In certain townships, a house is not subject to full taxation until it is completed. So if a wily and frugal houseowner were to maintain a useless extra door as evidence of his intention to add a further wing to his home, how could he be charged full tax? But a door in the corner of a house? Is this the product of a long-smoldering dispute within a family? Or of an injudicious last testament? Or the afterthought of an absent-minded architect?

35

36

In the Western world, doors commonly proclaim their owners' affluence and social status. In the East, while doors are points of great social significance, their message is immensely more subtle. For all the intensity of Japanese public life, for all the competitiveness that marks the Japanese approach to industry and trade, and indeed for all the violence that has emerged from these traits, the diametrically different Japanese attitudes towards home and private life is baffling to Westerners. The Japanese home, no matter how successful its owner, is as simple and serene as Japanese industry is complex and dynamic.

Buddhism is probably the most potent key to the Japanese home. Except in size and quality of materials there is little to distinguish the modest from the affluent home. There is a common yearning for a simple organic appearance, brought to perfection by infinitely patient attention to detail. The home and its entrance are moulded into the landscape. Natural woods, retaining their irregularity, tinted perhaps but never glossed over with paint, compose the door and are allowed to weather. No glazing or furtive peep-hole, but a grill of wooden slats, which permits the host to stand invisibly prepared for the significant ceremony of welcoming guests. And then within, worldly shoes left at the door, serene hours of uncluttered hospitality, calmed by glimpses of the ordered miniature garden outside.

A Canadian horse-breeder has a pair of white horses painted on his stable doors. Is it pure coincidence that in far-off India those identical images are considered protective, the symbols of power and fertility?

Christians in many parts of the world bedeck their doorways at Christmastime with wreaths of holly and sprigs of mistletoe, yet the custom derives from the pagan druids of ancient Britain, who revered such plants for their power to bring fertility and plenty. Corn-husks hung on the door at harvest-time are intended

40

41

42

43

to encourage a similar prosperity.

A broom left at the door is said to prevent a witch from entering the house. If a witch should make off with the broom, she may also remove any evil spells from the household. But if the same broom has been used to sweep dirt from the house over the threshold, it may well have brushed away the family's good luck.

Antlers or horns mounted over a hunting lodge door are not mere trophies; not only do they scare off evil spirits but they also ensure good hunting in the future.

44

45

A crescent moon with a star symbolizes paradise. But why does it appear on the door of an outdoor toilet in North America? In Eastern Europe toilet doors are marked "000", zero being the sign for potentiality and eternity.

Since doors mark the frontier between the familiar security of home and an outside world full of possible misfortunes and threats, it is not surprising that doors have always been the focus of superstitions, of traditional customs, and of protective symbols. Even the purely whimsical decoration of doors may reflect a long-held peasant belief that unmarked surfaces may be taken over by evil spirits.

Not all such customs relate to decoration. In certain countries doors are opened to ease the passing of a dying member of the family and those present must avoid standing or kneeling between the deathbed and the door. Elsewhere doors are opened to ease a difficult childbirth. In parts of the Orient the deceased are buried near the doors of homes to serve as guardian spirits, yet in England it used to be the custom when someone in the family died to unhinge and hide the

front gate and to take the body to the cemetery a roundabout way so that its ghost would not easily find its way back to the house.

A bride leaving her home must leave by the front door, stepping over the threshold with her right foot first, and when she has been married her husband must carry her across the threshold of her new home. In some communities it is considered unlucky ever to step on the threshold, in others to linger or to stumble or to sneeze at the threshold, to leave a door open, or to enter by one door and leave by another.

We may smile at such survivals of a primitive fear of the unknown, but how many of us have never taken some small ritual insurance against bad luck? Even Christians who believe God to be omnipotent have never quite discounted the possibility of a Devil almost as powerful, backed by a host of minor demons. The gorgon's heads that so often topped the columns of medieval doorways were not intended to cow godfearing visitors but rather to drive off spirits of malign intent. Similarly, while crosses decorating a gate might mark the entrance to a convent or church and might induce a pious response in passers-by, they could also serve to reinforce it against invasion by diabolical forces.

A horseshoe nailed on or above a door used to be one of the most common guarantees of good fortune in the Western world. It is said to derive from the legend that the English St. Dunstan, patron of the blind, spotted the Devil trying to sneak into his church. Adroitly he nailed the evil one to the doorpost by his hoof. When the Devil

50

51

pleaded for mercy, the saint agreed to release him on condition that he promise never to enter a doorway guarded by a hoof mark. There is said to be an added potency if the horseshoe is attached to the lintel by four nails on one side and three on the other, making up the lucky number seven; whether the open end of the shoe should face upwards or downwards has long been a matter of vehement debate.

The automobile, having driven horses from the roads, has so far provided no talisman equivalent to the horseshoe. But perhaps the pelicans and swans and other birds of good omen that nowadays grace suburban lawns and screen doors are thought of as protective symbols. Just in case.

Indeed so various have been the symbols and charms by which men have sought to guard their doors from unknown perils that almost any symbol or superstition will make you feel secure. As long as you believe it will protect you.

53

54

55

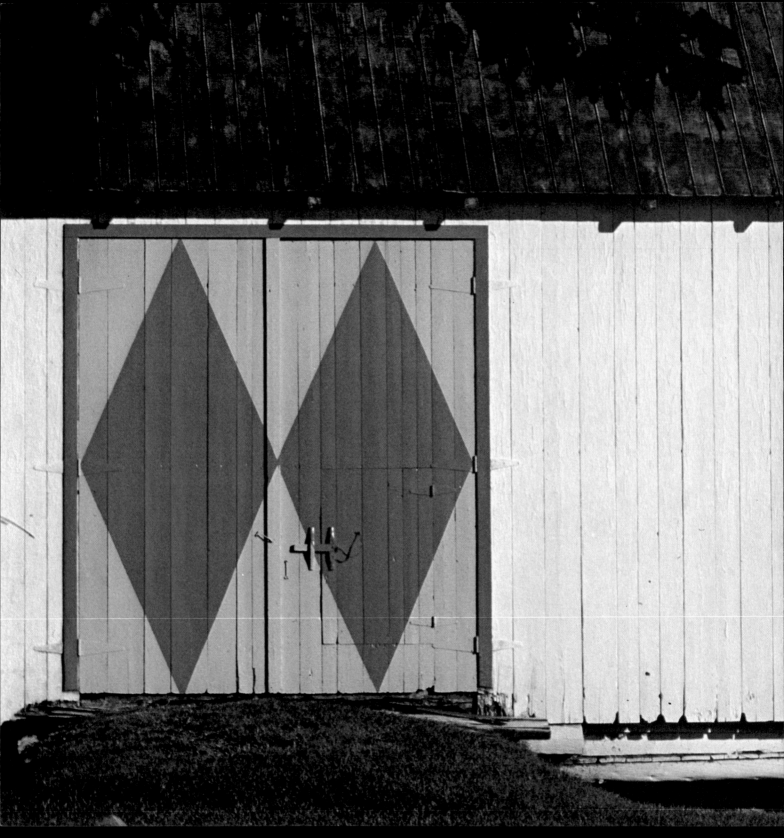

At the zenith of the civilizations created by Greece, Egypt and Rome, architecture took on an appropriate grandeur. Vast temples, tombs and public buildings were graced by doors of matching scale and magnificence. There are records of great ornate doors of marble, of wood and of hollowcast bronze, but while the ruins of these great monuments survive, little trace of the doors has been found. Throughout the Dark Ages in Europe regimes needed to defend rather than glorify themselves and their doors remained functional and sturdy. The Italian Renaissance and the imperial affluence of the Moors, the Spanish, and the French restored some of the classical glory to the building of doors, many of which have been preserved as architectural treasures today.

At a more modest domestic level, just as there are homeowners who use their doors to display their importance or their superstitions, so there are others who prefer their doors to reflect craftsmanship, or fashion, or even whimsy.

A beautiful front door, if it costs somewhat more than a fine suit of clothes, remains always on view to neighbors and passers-by and usually outwears more than one owner. Sculptors and woodcarvers are usually hungrier (and more gratified by display of their work) than are tailors, and they are invariably better schooled in the finest traditions of their craft.

59

60

61

Unfortunately in this century the fashion of uniformity has tended to favor the tailors rather than the sculptors.

Even in countries which have no classical tradition of art or which by tradition frown on ostentation, doors and doorways are graced with care and craftsmanship. Whatever is well-made, however simple and of the most rudimentary materials, reflects well on its owner. It need not, like a suburban home, be annually rejuvenated, for in such simple and uncompetitive communities it is acknowledged that a well-made door, like a good wine, improves with age.

Doors, because they are so important and so visible, have inevitably attracted sly satire, fantasy and artistic ingenuity. Even in medieval times the craftsmen who carved friezes of allegorical figures around the doorways of magnificent churches were notorious for working into the elaborate traceries caricatures of local dignitaries or of workmates against whom they held a grudge.

With far less scope, a Mexican workman, commissioned to paint a warehouse, turns the building into a

subtle optical joke. With a few simple strokes he makes the warehouse doors disappear.

And a bar owner, combining advertisement with wry offbeat humor, reverses the scale of things by making a keyhole a doorway.

The technology of glass and steel and preformed concrete is rapidly wiping out the possibility of such idiosyncrasy and humor. Indeed at the center of some of our cities discernible doors and windows have been eliminated. We walk glassy-eyed down sterile dazzling canyons of office towers. For that reason the ingenious artist who managed to compose from such unpromising materials a shopfront that is pure art deco deserves our passing applause.

We are conditioned by the slick uniformity that comprises much modern architecture. And so it is not surprising that our guide-books describe communities that have preserved their traditional character as "picture-book" towns and cities. Moreover, there is something disturbing about the fact that when we do visit such places, we tend to see them as artificial and contrived.

Contrived they may be, in the sense that traditional builders and craftsmen cared about details and about the impression their work would make, but artificial only if we

consider a cave the truly "natural" home. In Europe, particularly in Central and Eastern Europe, there has long survived a traditional love of architectural decoration, deriving perhaps from that superstitious peasant dread of open spaces, but just as probably and much more simply from a native liking for color and display, as a means of alleviating the dull and dispiriting aspects of country life.

There is a theatrical air about the facade of the country inn that seems to demand the frame of a proscenium arch; it could well be the setting for the opening scene of a Viennese or Hungarian light opera. The inn door, with its tiled and garlanded surround, could burst open, slightly shaking the whole facade, to release the handsome hero-tenor in his lederhosen and allow him to flirt melodiously with the drindl'd village girls of the chorus.

It is a decorative tradition not yet dead, vital enough to survive and with a fair chance of doing so, since the pall of uniformity is making more and more of us appreciative of whatever is picturesque and eccentric and lovingly made.

It need not be a whole dramatic facade; any fine detail, however small, can catch our delight—a quirky curvaceous fanlight; doorways wreathed in stylized glades or garlands; doors embellished with painted panels and frosted glass or crowned by glittering intricate tiles, doors that stop you in your tracks and invite you to enter.

67

68

69

SORGE DER VORMÜNDER · HEIN QUAST UND JACOB BRANT · DIESES NEUE WIEDER ERBAUET 1778 UND IST GERIC

45

71

73

74

Lock your door and keep your neighbors honest
English proverb

76

77

78

79

Doors, for all the ends to which they have been adapted, were primarily intended to provide security from intruders. There are still many communities, small and secluded for the most part, where householders boast with communal pride that they never bother to lock their doors. It is usually in these same communities that the main function of bolts, latches and locks is to keep livestock in rather than keep intruders out.

Country people share an easygoing attitude to doors and to security. There is no

80

great hurry about the daily round, so it is no problem that a weathered gate or door sags on its hinges and has to be slowly and laboriously eased open or shut. Factory-made bolts or hinges have to be fetched from the general store in town, so surely such hardware can be contrived from a few nails and screws and a scrap of wood. And if it works well enough, why go to the bother and expense of getting the real thing?

Never bolt a door with a boiled carrot
Irish proverb

81

82

83

84

85

86

87

When I was a lad I served a term
As an office boy to an Attorney's firm.
I cleaned the windows and I swept the floor,
And I polished up the handle on the big
front door.
I polished up that handle so carefully
That now I am the Ruler of the Queen's Navy.
W. S. Gilbert: *HMS Pinafore*

In cities, however, door fittings must not only secure the lives and possessions of the householders but must also secure their social standing. Handles, door-knockers and bell-pushes, if they are well-polished and of superior design, can do as much for the prestige of a house or professional establishment as an expensive, neatly-tied necktie might do for a man's image. Unlike many of the doors to which it is attached nowadays, door furniture is rarely

89

mass-produced; it tends to be made, in infinite variety, by small local manufacturers or foundries.

An unwelcome innovation is that electronic device set into the door-post into which the visitor must shout his name and business before the door is electrically unlocked. But there are still bells and door-knockers in use, by the design of which the house-owner may establish his status, and by the manipulation of which the visitor can signal both his character and his mood.

Only in the gates of antiquated convents do grilles

90

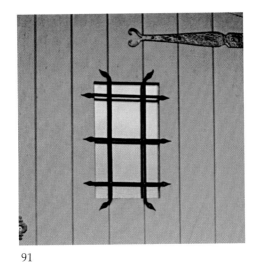

91

survive, and those in our relaxed times lack the romantic significance they had when Don Juans whispered escape to rich rebellious novitiates. There is little romance in viewing the eye of a romantic lover through the magnifying glass of a present-day spy-hole.

92

93

There are the doors we scarcely notice, of course, no matter how often we pass through them—the doors of familiar local stores. We are usually so intent on remembering what we need to buy, what quip or greeting we offer the friendly pharmacist or grocer, that only the warning tinkle of the bell that marks our entry reminds us that there is a door at all. Unless we arrive too late and are informed by the card hung inside its glazed panels that the store is "Closed". Then it becomes the most noticeable obstructive door in the world, stolid against our attempts to open

it, tauntingly revealing exactly what we intended to buy in the shadows within—yet no glimmer of light or sign of the store-keeper. We have now every reason to ignore such a door the next time we enter.

Barbershop doors should always be wide and open and on the shady side of the main street. With perhaps a curtain of beads or ribbons to keep out the flies—but not if that obscures a clear view of all that is happening outside, for what more easeful joy is there for a man than to be carefully shaved or barbered while watching the world go about its business?

Craftsmen's doors too should always be open. By law every curious child or inquisitive adult should be entitled to peer inside, smelling the sawdust and hot iron, enjoying the noise and bustle, seeing how barrel staves are sawn and moulded, how the hoops are shrunk on and the ends fitted. Or for that matter, how horses are shod, churchbells are cast, or books are bound. As long as there are barrels and horses and bells and books around.

When they have disap-peared, all we will have left to wonder at is what lies behind the sullen obdurate doors of windowless warehouses. Occasionally when the many-wheeled leviathans of the freeways back in at dusk and the doors grind back on their rusty rollers, we are allowed to glimpse a shadowy interior mountain of unin-formative crates, to see them hefted forward by whining forklifts, and to hear the rumble of loading and the final clank of the tailgate. The monster snarls and roars, and

lumbers off towards the night and the freeway. Already the door has ground to a close, and we are left staring at the ''No Parking'' sign and wondering what is in there.

The fact remains that doors seem incomplete without activity. Windows are essentially static, to be looked into or out of, but doors need to be walked through. They are there to allow arrival and departure, and if they do not serve that purpose they might as well be windows or even just walls.

The proverb may advise us to lock our doors and keep our neighbors honest. Another cautions that an open door may tempt a saint. But it could be argued with equal point that a closed and bolted door may tempt a sinner. It is not beyond possibility that fewer burglars are motivated by avarice than by curiosity, or at least by the challenge issued by the locks and bolts of closed doors.

The most popular
coffee-house in
Lisbon, where seats
are rarely empty and where
lively conversation and
strong sweet coffee mingle
freely throughout every day,
probably owes its popularity
in large part to the inviting
generous proportions of the
graceful open doorway. Only
the obsessively diligent
passer-by could resist its invitation, with the added seduc-
tion of murmuring talk and
rich aroma that wafts over the
sidewalk.

104

All open doors are seductive, and when the sun is out and time slows down, the superstitions that warn against lingering on thresholds are invariably forgotten. Children play hide-and-seek while their parents casually pass the time of day with a friendly merchant. A family holds idle council in the gentle waning sunlight with the day's work done and the evening meal over. The threshold is the hearth of the summertime.

105

If you are old or if the season has brought work to a pause, what better grand-stand than a doorstep—there to join the acquaintances of a lifetime and ruminate on the perversities of the weather, the iniquities of the govern-ment, the way things were, and the idle ways of women-folk.

Meanwhile, across the street, as neighbor helps neighbor to fix her hair, neither feels that a chance to watch the ways of the world should be wasted in the dull privacy of a back room. Open doors are meant for open eyes.

107

Open doors provide the family album of a neighborhood. As we stroll along the streets, doorways frame snapshots far more natural than those caught self-consciously before the hypnotizing camera. A pair of neighbors rapt in gossip, father and son in rigid confrontation in a hallway, an old woman on a front step bowed in remembrance of some long-past joy or sorrow. We dare not stop and stare, for that would be an intrusion and would break the spell. But a glimpse out of a corner of the eye is enough to print the snapshot on the mind; we can develop it as we stroll, speculating on what had so absorbed those neighbors, on what misunderstanding had set son against father, on what moment of so many years ago the old woman was brooding.

There are two sides to an open door. We can linger in our own doorways and watch the mystery movie of the street. Why is this neighbor hurrying in that direction at this time of day? Who is that stranger strolling by? Who would he be visiting? And all the better if you have a screen door to veil your curiosity. And keep out the bugs and flies, of course.

Because they have framed those arrivals and departures that mark every lifetime with sadness or happiness, doorways stand out more vividly in our memories than other parts of home or workplace. A son setting off for a distant war, a daughter apprehensive in her finery for the church and then a new home of her own. The shadow of a changed half-remembered friend suddenly falling across the threshold; even the eager daily return of children from school, hungry and rambunctious . . . These are all recalled, as visibly as when they happened, as you stand now in that self-same doorway.

It may be the doorway you went to day after day to watch the sky, hoping to see the rainclouds that might save a parched crop. Or better the doorway from which you could see your husband and sons harvesting, gauging the time, from the angle of the sunlight past the eaves, when you should carry out the noonday meal. The doorway from which you watched for the doctor coming along the road, the same doorway from which you heard the thin cry of your firstborn in the bedroom within, at which you

welcomed guests for the christening, and then the doctor again, and another thin yell; that day it was raining and the boy was beside you eager to know if he had a brother or a sister...

Now there are only the marks on the doorpost, where you measured their heights as the years went by. They have their own doorways now. Soon perhaps they'll be bringing their children to see where they grew up, and you'll be waiting for their arrival at this same door.

Yes, the years are measured out at doorways.

113

I am the door.

Gospel According to St. John,
Chapter 9

116

117

118

Horses are indifferent to doors. If there's hay in their stalls, they'd just as soon stand head to the wall and munch it. If not, they may stand in the doorway and remind someone that it's coming up to feeding time. Or maybe they'll watch the less noble animals making fools of themselves around the barnyard.

Chickens have no patience with doors or gates. When they're inside one they are frantically certain that outside the ground is thick with scraps and grains, theirs for the pecking. And glistening thick worms writhing helpless on the grass, that the crows and pigeons will steal. When they're out, chickens will go to any lengths not to go back inside. They know they'll be expected to settle down and lay. They'd sooner lay around.

Cats despise doors. They know that no house is proof against their stealth; there will always be a transom they can reach, or a window ajar. And besides if they pretend to sleep on the doorstep in the sun, a silly bird may hop too close.

A door is what a dog is perpetually on the wrong side of.

Ogden Nash:

"A Dog's Best Friend Is His Illiteracy"

Country doors do not have to seem other than they are. They are built to endure, and to serve practical purposes, not to impress. Farmers generally share a liking for what fits in with the nature of the countryside. Wood that looks like wood, even if it needs to be soaked in preservative, but not wood glossed over with paint; wood that will show its grain and strength, retaining some memory of when it stood as one of a proud stand of trees

before it was felled and hauled off to the sawmill.

Wood that you can still almost feel the life in as you lean on the half-door of the barn in the evening. A great good door, well made by your own hands. Heavy enough nearly to break your back these chill mornings when you have to let the cows out to pasture; it will probably begin to sag soon like the doors on the older outhouses. But no matter, a door that you'll always be proud of, that'll long keep the weather out and the cattle in.

121

122

125

126

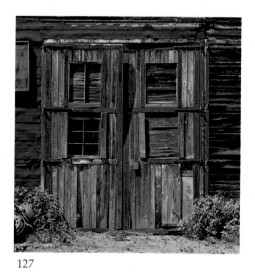

127

128

As farming becomes less a way of life than an operation of business, such doors as these, roughly etched with the story of hundreds of seasons, are likely to become curiosities. With doomsday warnings forever sounding of future global shortages of food, smaller older farmsteads are being engulfed into what are dully described as economically viable agricultural units. The old buildings are bulldozed down and the venerable wood of their doors and walls and roofs is either burned or sold to a city jobber who can sell it at a tidy profit as decor for some modish cocktail lounge or restaurant.

Even on those small farms that do manage to survive, those original sturdy doors that are still in use are likely to be the last of their kind. The men who knew how to make them are either dead now or too old to begin again. And with the farm-belts long ago cleared of woodland, the lumber needed would be too expensive. When eventually they have rotted beyond repair, such doors will have to be replaced by lighter machine-made doors of metal or fiberboard that will swing easily and efficiently on their hinges but will have no story written upon them of how the land was cleared and how a farm was built on it and how its doors served a family through their years and grew old gracefully with the man who made them.

We must eat of course, and prosper, but can we live to the full if we close the door on all else?

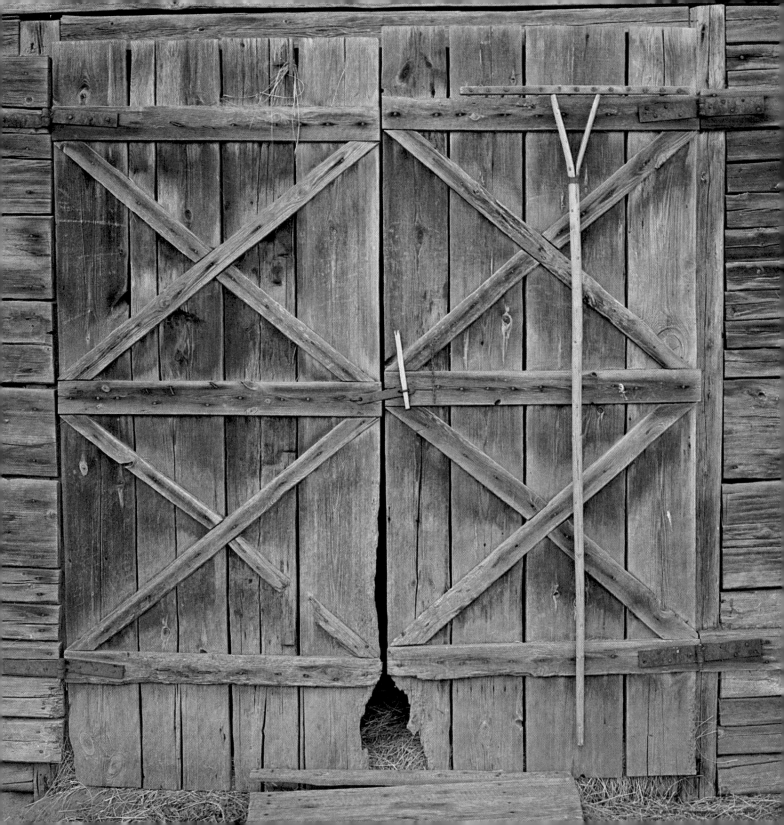

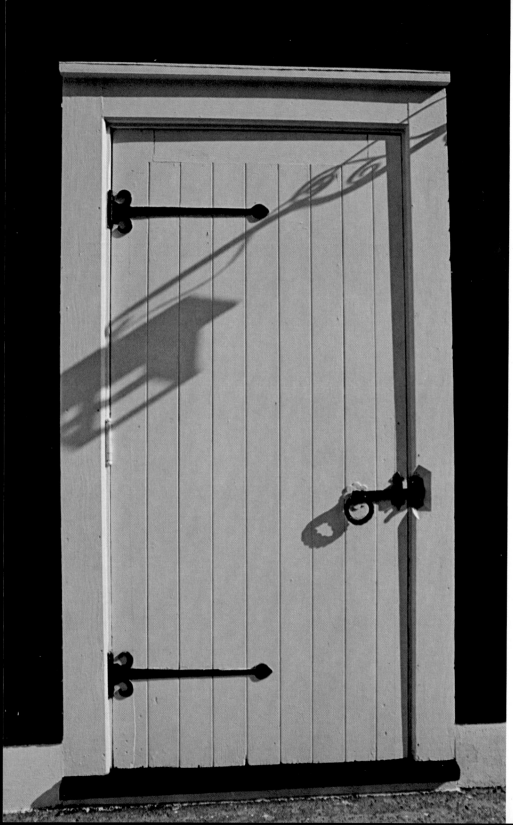

*Men shut their doors against
a setting sun.*
William Shakespeare: *Timon of Athens*

Already the iron door of
the north
Clangs open: birds, leaves,
snows
Order their populations forth,
And a cruel wind blows.
Stanley Kunitz: *End of Summer*

133

132

134

I have been here before,
But when or how I cannot tell;
I know the grass beyond
the door,
The sweet keen smell . . .

Dante Gabriel Rossetti: *Sudden Light*

The English have always placed a great value on privacy and on the sanctity of the home. "An Englishman's home," so the saying goes, "is his castle." And even if the English home did lack battlements and a moat, its door was usually imposing and solid enough to deter presumptuous intruders. The English classical doorway of the nineteenth century, when class distinctions began to take on monumental proportions, was quite as explicit in its message as the medieval castle gate with its coat of arms. If its Georgian proportions, its elegance and dignity were not enough to impress, there was usually a plaque nearby announcing "No Hawkers, Peddlers, Or Tradesmen". These underlings were consigned to a "Tradesman's Entrance" at the rear or side of the mansion, or possibly down a narrow flight of steps at basement level, there to be rebuffed by a member of the household's domestic staff. Even social equals could not merely drop in for a chat. An afternoon tea or luncheon had to be preceded by a calling card, with a subtle inscription, deposited on the silver salver of the footman who swung open the splendid if formidable door. An invitation might return.

It would possibly have perturbed the Christian English gentleman who owned such a doorway that the noble columns that flanked it derived from primitive dwellings that were constructed of bundles of reeds, or that the spokes of its arched fanlight were possibly related to pagan sun-worship. Since the English upper classes, schooled in Greek and Latin, considered Rome the inspiration for their own imperial affluence, they were less

perturbed by the fact that their doorways drew also from Greco-Roman classical design.

The Georgian doorway established itself wherever English commerce made its mark: in Boston, New York, Philadelphia, and Dublin. In the American South, where porches and verandas were a climatic imperative, the style reverted to variations of the more expansive Palladian style.

In Europe over the same period the doorways of the

rich, long beset by war and civic strife, were far less arrogant in their design. Even when they allowed themselves the extravagance of double leaves, there was a defensiveness in the glazed upper panels guarded by strong grilles of decorative ironwork.

As well as privacy, the English valued a measure of conformity. Those haughty Georgian doorways in London and Dublin were usually set in the continuous facades of town house

139

140

terraces and crescents and
while at first glance they give
an impression of uniformity,
they were permitted never-
theless a wide variety of detail
in their frames, panelling and
fittings.

Such doors were built to
endure. But there are no
longer English gentlemen
rich enough to maintain the
vast houses behind them as
town residences, and there
are no longer footmen to
sweep them open and receive
calling cards. Instead they
now house smaller branches

143

of the civil service, or the managements of public utilities, or professional associations, or they are divided up between medical specialists and fashionable dentists. But the gleaming overweening doors maintain their air of privacy and impassive gentility.

Georgian doorways, even after the decline and fall of the British Empire, maintain a stiff upper lip.

144

145

148

149

150

151

Open doors and gate-
ways are promises.
They imply progress,
discovery. Instead of
rejection they offer us an
invitation, if not to enter at
least to look.

Architects of real vision
never use doorways merely to
exclude or divide; they so
arrange them that they serve
to focus attention on some
vista of grace or beauty
beyond, framing another
doorway, or a glimpse of
garden, an enticing succes-
sion of rooms, or the upward
spiral of a stairway. Their

doorways never bring us to a stop; they reveal another prospect.

Those of us obliged to live in large modern cities may contemplate such perfection with some sense of despair. We may live in a highrise apartment block, a veritable monument to security from its electronically-controlled entrance to its sullen corridors of closed doors. We may feel besieged, if not imprisoned, and may envy those lucky enough to own ample houses in the landscaped suburbs. And

those in the suburbs, trapped by taxes and rising costs and the need to keep pace with their neighbors' apparent affluence, yearn to escape to a small farm in the country where they could grow their own food. And those still on the farms, meanwhile, long for those times past when farm life was simple and serene and self-sufficient. But of course the one doorway through which there is no escape is the doorway to the past, and what we may feel we glimpse there is largely illusion.

It should never be forgotten that doors were originally conceived as a means of defense, in fear of a limitless unknown world, of savage animals, and of lurking human enemies. During long periods of the thousands of years since, men have been obliged continually to bar their door against barbarism, plague, war, revolution, crime, persecution, and their own superstitious bugbears.

There have been periods of history that may seem in retrospect to have been more stable and less troubled than our own times, but the glimpses we allow ourselves of such idyllic times are never fulfilled by close examination.

Invariably the stability and comfort and beauty were the privileges of a small élite. In ancient China, where the first extensive civilization flourished, the ornate homes of the nobility were in sharp contrast to the hovels where the mass of peasants struggled to survive. Yet those noble homes had to be built in accordance with a rigid set of superstitions and customs, the siting of their doors and windows governed not by comfort or convenience but by the need to ward off evil spirits and to be properly aligned with the cosmos; even the simple ushering of a guest through the doorways involved a slow and elaborate ritual.

Much as we may admire the majesty of Egypt's tombs and palaces, we should remember that the suitable interment of a pharaoh probably cost the lives of thousands of slaves, some sealed up behind the tombs' vast stone doors to serve their masters on the journey to eternity.

In imperial Rome slaves ensured that patricians could savour life in their opulent villas, with their doors opening to a vista of inner courtyards, cooled by pools and fountains and shaded by trees. But the mass of Rome's plebians lived in multistoried blocks that were bleak even by the frugal standards of our own public housing. The indentured laborers and craftsmen who raised and ornamented the magnificent church doorways of the

Middle Ages were not even as well housed as the Romans. And within the impressive doorways of Moorish and Mongol palaces were other doorways that rarely opened, behind which the womenfolk lived out their whole lives in service to their masters.

Whatever misgivings we may have about our world, we must be aware that more of us are in a position to involve ourselves in improving it than ever before in human history. When rigid superstition, slavery, serfdom, and the treatment of

women as chattels became
abuses too heavy to be en-
dured, the means were some-
how found to bring them to
an end. The doorway out of
any human problem has yet
to prove permanently closed.

More and more of us than
ever before have doors we can
call our own. We can come
and go as we please. And if we
feel our doors are unworthy
of us, we mostly have the
means and the leisure to re-
place them. If we notice our
doors, that is, since doors are
amongst those meaningful
features of life that we see

156

often and notice seldom.

But we are beginning to notice such details. In many cities people are rallying to resist the destruction of older graceful buildings and their replacement with featureless towers of steel and glass. We need buildings and doorways beside which we can reasonably measure ourselves.

But there are other doors, at a time when it is easier than ever before for men to communicate and to relate, that are continually being slammed and locked. Doors that imperceptibly imprison us and divide us. They are doors reinforced and locked by our fears, superstitions, pride, and prejudices, and only we ourselves can unlock and open them and allow those outside an inviting glimpse of whatever grace, beauty, promise, and humanity we have built within ourselves.

My secrets cry aloud,
I have no need of tongue.
My heart keeps open house,
My doors are widely flung.
Theodore Roethke: "Open House"

Photographs

Photographers

Val Clery was born and grew up in
Dublin. Following wartime service as
a commando, he worked as a writer
and broadcaster in Ireland, in Britain
and in Canada, where he now lives.
He was founding editor of the period-
ical *Books in Canada* and has written
for Canada's leading newspapers and
magazines. His other books include
an anthology of Canadian non-fiction
and *Windows*, the companion volume to
Doors.